What Is That?

A Book about Question Marks

by Marie Powell
illustrated by Anthony Lewis

amicus readers 3

Say Hello to Amicus Readers.

You'll find our helpful dog, Amicus, chasing a ball—to let you know the reading level of a book.

1

Learn to Read
Frequent repetition, high frequency words, and close photo-text matches introduce familiar topics and provide support for brand new readers.

2

Read Independently
Some repetition is mixed with varied sentence structures and a select amount of new vocabulary words are introduced with text and photo support.

3

Read to Know More
Interesting facts and engaging art and photos give fluent readers fun books both for reading practice and to learn about new topics.

Amicus Readers are published by Amicus
P.O. Box 1329, Mankato, MN 56002
www.amicuspublishing.us

Illustrations by Anthony Lewis

Produced for Amicus by The Peterson Publishing Company and Red Line Editorial.

Editor Jenna Gleisner
Designer Jake Nordby

Printed in Malaysia
10 9 8 7 6 5 4 3 2 1

Library of Congress Cataloging-in-Publication Data
Powell, Marie, 1958-
  What is that? : a book about question marks / by Mar
Powell ; illustrations by Anthony Lewis.
    pages cm. -- (Punctuation Station)
  Summary: Tyson, Emma, and Paul build silly snowmen
and play in the snow, while teaching each other how to
correctly use question marks in a sentence.
  ISBN 978-1-60753-732-8 (library binding)
  ISBN 978-1-60753-836-3 (ebook)
  1. English language--Punctuation--Juvenile literature.
Lewis, Anthony, illustrator. II. Title.
  PE1450.P69 2015
  421'.1--dc23
                                        2014045819

Punctuation marks help us understand writing. A question mark at the end of a sentence shows when someone asks a question.

What will Tyson, Jane, and Paul do after school today?

At lunchtime, Paul hands Jane and Tyson a note.

"Let me know your answer after lunch," says Paul.

"What does he want an answer to?" asks Jane. "I don't see a question in his note."

play after school

After lunch, Jane asks Paul, "Did you mean to ask us to play after school?"

"Yes! I forgot the question mark. Let me rewrite it," says Paul.

After school, Jane and Paul pile up snow.

"What is that?" asks Tyson.

"A snowman," says Jane.

"Where is its head?" asks Tyson.

"And where is its nose?" asks Tyson.

"We don't have a carrot. Paul, will you hand me those rocks?" asks Jane.

Paul lies down and swipes his arms and legs across the snow.

"What are you doing?" Tyson asks.

"I'm making a snow angel," says Paul. "Can you both make one?"

Next, Tyson builds a round fort with blocks of snow.

"Now what is that?" Paul asks.

"It's an igloo," says Tyson. "Do you want to come inside?"

Remember to use a question mark:

To show when someone is asking a question:
"What is that?"

To show when someone asks for something:
"Will you hand me those rocks?" asks Jane.